INDEX

T0001180

CHANGE YOUR CULTURE TO CHANGE YOUR COMPANY

How would you like to **increase** your company's net **profitability** by up to **71%?**

How about **increasing** your company's net **profitability** by up to **756%?**

THIS IS POSSIBLE. I AM NOT KIDDING!

THIS BOOK WILL SHOW YOU HOW

IN 1992 IBM was in serious trouble and on the verge of declaring bankruptcy. Desperate to survive, they brought in a new CEO named Lou Gerstner in a last-ditch effort to save the company. Lou did save IBM. Then, he wrote a book about his experience called *"Who Says Elephants Can't Dance?"*

HERE IS WHAT HE SAID ABOUT COMPANY CULTURE:

Until I came to IBM, I probably would have told you that Culture was just one among several important elements in any organization's makeup and success - along with vision, strategy, marketing, financials, and the like...

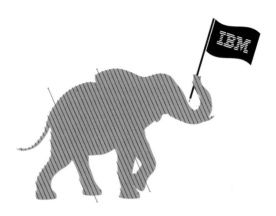

 In my time at IBM, I came to see that Culture isn't just one aspect of the game, it is the game. In the end, an organization is nothing more than the collective capacity of its people to create value.

~ Lou Gerstner, Who Says Elephants Can't Dance

SIMPLY, IF YOU DON'T CHANGE THE CULTURE, YOU WON'T CHANGE THE COMPANY!

LET THE CULTURE SHAPING BEGIN

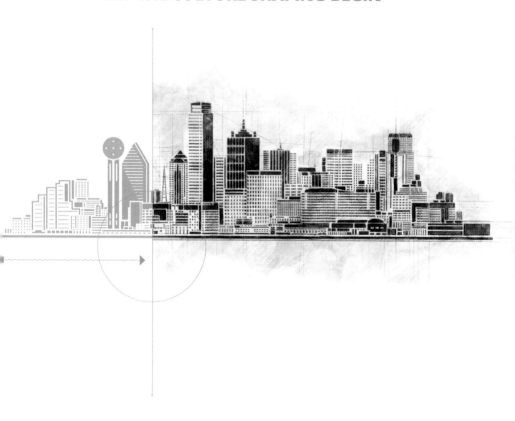

CRAC
FO

IDENTIFY
KS IN THE
NDATION

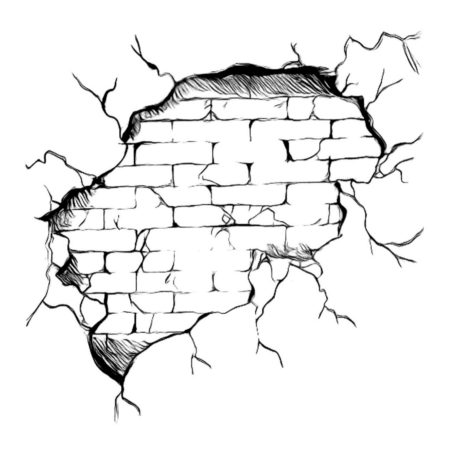

THE QUALITY OF YOUR COMPANY CULTURE IS DIRECTLY REFLECTED IN YOUR

BOTTOM LINE, PROFITABILITY, AND MARKET DOMINANCE.

If Company Culture showed up on a profit and loss statement, it would be the first data point looked at by all executives.

WHEN EXECUTIVES PAY ATTENTION TO THE SEVERE NEGATIVE IMPACT OF LOW ENGAGEMENT, THEY WILL FOCUS ON INCREASING ENGAGEMENT IMMEDIATELY.

LOW EMPLOYEE ENGAGEMENT IS EXPEN$IVE.

DO THE MATH

What percentage of highly engaged employees (HEE) do you have?

01 Multiply the number of **highly engaged employees** (HEE) at your company by **100**.

02 Divide the answer by the **total number of employees** (TE) you have.

THIS WILL GIVE YOU THE PERCENTAGE OF HIGHLY ENGAGED EMPLOYEES AT YOUR COMPANY.

FORMULA: $$\frac{HEE \times 100}{TE} = HEE\%$$

TO UNDERSTAND the amount of profit you are *actively losing from a lack of engagement*, simply subtract HEE from 100. This number shows you the percentage of unengaged employees and therefore the profit you are <u>leaving on the table</u>.

FORMULA

HEE% - 100 **PROFIT PERCENTAGE ACTIVELY LOST**

The percentage of disengaged employees is reflected in

- Lost profitability
- Lost productivity
- Lost innovation
- Lost agility
- Lost competitive advantage

and much MORE!

LOW EMPLOYEE ENGAGEMENT IS A MASSIVE SILENT TAX ON YOUR COMPANY OR ORGANIZATION.

GALLUP REVEALS YEAR AFTER YEAR THAT THE AVERAGE ENGAGEMENT RATE AT A TYPICAL U.S. COMPANY IS
29%.

GLOBALLY, IT IS 15%.

THIS MEANS THAT EITHER 71% TO 85% OF THE WORKFORCE SUCKS OR, WHATEVER IS GOING ON AT THE COMPANY IS NOT ENGAGING.

SIDE NOTE: When I do keynotes at conferences for a wide range of industries, I ask C-Level Executives and Managers from companies of varying sizes what they think the average engagement rate at a company is. I hear percentages MUCH lower than the Gallup poll shows.

I HEAR NUMBERS AS LOW AS 2%!

IN CONTRAST...

One Harvard Study showed that companies who create remarkable Company Cultures saw an increase upwards of **756% in net profitability** over the course of a mere 10 years.

QUIT WORRYING ABOUT HEADCOUNT AND START FOCUSING ON

"HEAD IN THE GAME" COUNT.

How many of your employees truly have their focus on the company's GOALS?

LOW EMPLOYEE ENGAGEMENT IS THE BIGGEST INDICATOR THAT A COMPANY'S CULTURE IS BROKEN.

REGARDLESS of the baseline quality of workers, an engaged workforce is going to be more successful than an apathetic workforce.

LET'S PUT THIS IDEA INTO PRACTICE...

USED TO MEAN
"PIECE OF CRAP"

IT MOST CERTAINLY DOES *NOT* MEAN THAT TODAY.

WHAT CHANGED ?

Multiple things from Wyoming, but one HUGE factor was quality guru, Edwards Deming and a group of Japanese managers who were committed to making a change.

DEMING WAS FANATICAL ABOUT HIS BELIEF THAT PEOPLE WERE NOT THE PROBLEM.
THE FLAWED PROCESS WAS THE PROBLEM.

- Put people in a **broken** system and they will perform **ineffectively.**
- Put people in an **effective** system and they will perform **effectively.**

DEMING was largely ignored in the U.S. In contrast, war-torn and desperate to rebuild, Japan was very intrigued by Deming's work. Deming went to Japan and, alongside Japanese management, revolutionized their manufacturing at every single level.

THE
RESULT

HIGHLY ENGAGED EMPLOYEES PRODUCING HIGH QUALITY RESULTS

LOW EMPLOYEE ENGAGEMENT IS NOT AN EMPLOYEE PROBLEM.

IT IS A **COMPANY CULTURE** PROBLEM.

A PROBLEM THAT YOU CAN FIX.

IT'S TIME TO STOP MOANING about low engagement and start focusing on architecting a Company Culture that actively empowers every person at your company to act like an **owner.**

THERE IS A LOT OF WEATHER IN NORTH TEXAS TODAY.

I WAS DRIVING IN DALLAS LISTENING TO THE RADIO AND I HEARD THE WEATHER PERSON SAY THIS...

NEWS FLASH there is **"weather"** everywhere, every day.

JUST LIKE EVERY PLACE HAS WEATHER,
EVERY COMPANY HAS A **CULTURE.**

DAVID FOSTER WALLACE

illustrates this point in his famous Kenyon College commencement speech, "This is Water." Foster opens his address to the graduating class of 2005 with an anecdote about two fish swimming through the ocean.

There are these two young fish swimming along and they happen to meet an older fish swimming the other way. The older fish nods at them and says, 'Morning, boys. How's the water?' The two young fish swim on for a bit and then eventually one of them looks over at the other fish and asks, 'What the hell is water?' [1]

1: To read the full transcript of David Foster Wallace's keynote, visit https://fs.blog/2012/04/david-foster-wallace-this-is-water/

IN A COMPANY, YOUR CULTURE IS THE WATER. EVERYONE IS SWIMMING IN IT ALL THE TIME WHETHER THEY ARE AWARE OF IT OR NOT.

It is unlikely that anyone in the company is consciously aware of the water they're swimming in. As a leader, it is your responsibility to enlighten the rest of the team to the water around them and ensure that the water contributes to the company's success. It is the responsibility of a leader to identify your company's water and craft it into an effective Culture.

**WHAT THINGS MAKE
UP THE WATER IN
YOUR COMPANY?**

GREAT
CULTURES

- **GREAT CULTURES SEPARATE TOP TIER COMPANIES FROM LOSERS.**
- **GREAT CULTURES ARE NOT INHERITED, BUT BUILT.**
- **GREAT CULTURES ARE EASILY IDENTIFIED.**

TRUE OR FALSE

COMPANY CULTURE IS ETHEREAL AND NOT REALLY TANGIBLE.[2]

2: CEO Dave told me that "'Company Culture' is a made up term by some consultant to sell more business." Insert massive eye roll by m

FALSE

Just like architecting a building for maximum efficiency, you can architect a specific and defined Company Culture for maximum engagement, performance, and profitability.

**TO BEGIN ARCHITECTING A CULTURE,
WE FIRST NEED TO UNDERSTAND CULTURE.**

CULTURE IS...

THE PREVAILING VALUES, BELIEFS, BEHAVIORS, AND LANGUAGE THAT PERMEATE AND DEFINE YOUR COMPANY.

The beliefs and feelings people have about the company, produce their actions which **create the results you SEE.**

HOW DO YOU KNOW WHAT THE PEOPLE AT YOUR COMPANY BELIEVE AND FEEL?

LOOK AT THEIR ACTIONS

(Seriously – go walk around and **LOOK!**)

WHAT DO YOU OBSERVE?

People not speaking up in meetings.

Having high turnover.

People rarely recruiting for your company.

Having silos or worse yet, war camps.

Having low engagement.

People living for the weekend.

OR

People giving discretionary effort.

Having actionable ideas abound.

High energy in your hallways.

Collaboration for the good of the enterprise as a whole.

People constantly referring their friends to work for your company.

People enjoying work!

GREAT COMPANY CULTURES

- ADDRESS BELONGING
- MAXIMIZE ENGAGEMENT
- PROPEL PERFORMANCE
- IGNITE THE SPIRIT
- PRODUCE OUTCOMES, NOT ACTIVITY
- PRESENT CHALLENGE AND FUN

T H I N K

RE-READ THE LIST.
HOW MANY OF THESE DOES YOUR
CURRENT COMPANY CULTURE ACCOMPLISH?

WHEN YOU IDENTIFY THE FLAWS IN THE FOUNDATION

YOU CAN BEGIN to address the **root cause** of your company's lack of engagement, efficiency, and overall success.

So now I've identified the flaws within my company, but HOW do I fix my company and architect the ideal Company Culture?

HOW DO I CREATE A COMPANY OF OWNERS?

GLAD YOU ASKED!

THE BASIC OUTLINE OF YOUR CULTURE BEGINS TO TAKE SHAPE

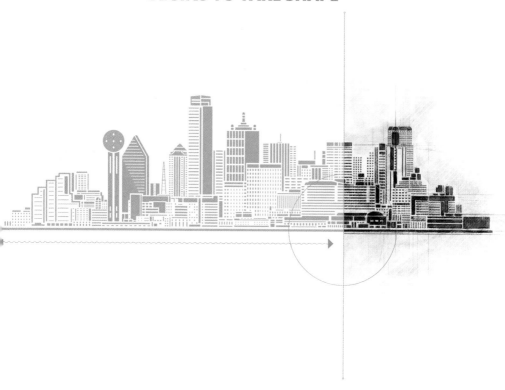

BLUE

PRINTING YOUR CULTURE

LET'S ARCHITECT A GREAT COMPANY CULTURE.

In the following few pages we are going to craft a blueprint for an immediately applicable and easy to follow process to architect your Company Culture. The Culture within your company is the blueprint for everything your company does.

THE 4 C'S OF CULTURE ARCHITECTING WILL GUIDE YOU THROUGH YOUR BLUEPRINTING PROCESS.

EACH OF THESE **C'S** REPRESENT A STEP IN THIS HOW-TO GUIDE AS YOU REINVENT, REIMAGINE, AND REINVIGORATE YOUR COMPANY CULTURE.

STICKS
AND
STONES

A blueprint is wonderful, but without the necessary tools to build your Culture, it will only sit as a great idea, never executed. Within each step, you will also learn a tool that is necessary to execute the blueprint for your company.

C1

CALL IT...

BY THE RIGHT NAME

THE BEGINNING OF WISDOM IS
CALLING THINGS BY THE RIGHT NAME

CHINESE PROVERB

If you know the enemy and know yourself, you need not fear the result of a hundred battles. If you know yourself but not the enemy, for every victory you will also suffer a defeat.

If you know neither the enemy nor yourself, you will succumb in every battle.

MANY COMPANIES AND LEADERS ARE IN ABSOLUTE DENIAL ABOUT THE STATE OF THEIR COMPANY.

For example, a survey conducted by William Schiemann revealed that **only 14% of employees** know their companies' strategy.

I have talked to many top executives whose perception of their organization is inconsistent with the perceptions of team members who are **"closer to the valve."**

AS A *leader* WHEN IT COMES TO CULTURE,

WHICH OF THE FOLLOWING ARE YOU?

OSTRICH

YOUR HEAD IS IN THE SAND CONVEYING ...

- This is somebody else's job.
- I don't really understand it, so I just ignore it.
- We're fine, really we are.
- I am sure our Culture is good, right?

PEACOCK

WE ARE AWESOME! BUT IN REALITY …

- It is all flash and no substance.
- There is a big gap between Leadership's assessment of the Culture and the assessment of those closest to the valve (Frontline workers).
- You don't know what you don't know.

BEAVER

REAL TANGIBLE ACTIVITY TO BUILD AND ENHANCE THE CULTURE ...

- Multiple levels of involvement from a cross-section of the company.
- Pride in the Culture across the board.
- Agreement between Leadership and Frontline workers about the state of the Culture.
- Culture is a top priority.

IS FOR CULTURE

CEO, COO, CFO, CHRO, CIO, CMO, CISO, etc.
the **C** no longer stands for **"CHIEF".**

IT STANDS FOR
"CULTURE".

THIS SHOULD BE THE TOP PRIORITY OF EVERY
EXECUTIVE TEAM MEMBER!

STATED CULTURE

- HOW A COMPANY SAYS THEY OPERATE
- WHAT A COMPANY SAYS THEY VALUE
- HOW A COMPANY SAYS THEY BEHAVE

THE DISPARITY BETWEEN THE STATED AND THE HIDDEN CULTURE SHOWS THE AMOUNT OF DYSFUNCTION IN A COMPANY

HIDDEN CULTURE

- HOW A COMPANY ACTUALLY OPERATES
- WHAT A COMPANY ACTUALLY VALUES
- HOW A COMPANY ACTUALLY BEHAVES

IS YOUR COMPANY CULTURE DYSFUNCTIONAL?

BEFORE YOU ANSWER, YOU NEED TO GO FIND OUT!

TAKE NOTES AS YOU GO.

GET OUT

INTERACT WITH THE PHYSICAL ATMOSPHERE. TAKE A WALK IN YOUR COMPANY'S ENVIRONMENT. BREATHE IN THE ESSENCE OF THE SPACE.

ASK YOURSELF:

01 What is clearly present?

02 What is obviously missing?

03 What is the range of moods I experience as I interact with the space?

04 What is the range of moods I observe in my team members?

05 How logical and efficient is the layout?

06 How attractive and comfortable is it?

07 What else do I notice?

⇥ GET IN

ASK

01 What is your name, position, and length of time with the company?

02 What challenges do you face at work?

03 What tangible changes would make this an even better place to work?

04 What do you love about working here?

05 Give a quick survey: How fulfilled are you on a scale from 1 to 10; 1 being the WORST place to work and 10 being the BEST place to work.

06 What else would you like to tell us about our company?

GET CURIOUS

ASK 10-20 PEOPLE IN VARIOUS PARTS OF YOUR
COMPANY THE FOLLOWING QUESTIONS.
(IF TRUST IS LOW, YOU MAY WANT TO USE AN ONLINE
SURVEY TO ALLOW FOR ANONYMITY AND HONESTY.)

AT OUR COMPANY

01 What do we say we do, that we actually do not do?

02 What do we say we do not do, that we actually do?

03 How big is the gap between our stated mission, values, and identity vs. how we actually operate?

WHY THIS TOP TALENT COMPANY LEADER WALKED OUT THE DOOR REALLY

I was engaged with a multi-billion dollar company assisting them in advancing an initiative. I was there one week each month and had an office next to the CEO. I was given free rein to do what I deemed necessary to achieve their goals.

At first, the initiative was not gaining traction.

One employee told me ...

Daren, I have been here 28 years, how many new initiatives do you think I have seen in that time? 28!

To generate the kind of urgency and interest I was looking for, I began teaching the S-Curve to different groups within the company. **The S-Curve is the life cycle of any business. It starts with a learning curve, then continues to progress into upward growth.** If you are not continuing to reinvent yourself, your company's growth will peak and then curve downward to obsolescence.

LIFE CYCLE OF ANY COMPANY
OR NEW ENDEAVOR

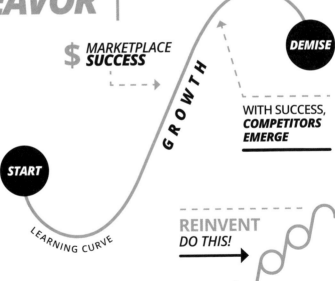

WITHOUT GROWTH, CHANGE, AND REINVENTING... YOU WILL PEAK!

$ MARKETPLACE *SUCCESS*

G R O W T H

DEMISE

WITH SUCCESS, *COMPETITORS EMERGE*

START

LEARNING CURVE

REINVENT *DO THIS!*

ONE MONTH I showed up at the company and was informed that one of their highest performers had resigned. They had promised this person a fast track road to success and the opportunity to create his own future in the company, so I was surprised that he would leave this opportunity for a position at a much smaller company.

I ASKED IF I COULD HAVE AN EXIT INTERVIEW WITH HIM. THE CEO RESPONDED, "WE HAVE ALL TALKED TO HIM AND KNOW WHY HE IS LEAVING BUT OF COURSE DAREN, DO WHATEVER YOU WANT."

The reasons this top performer gave the CEO and others for leaving were the typical excuses – he wanted to be closer to home, spend more time with family, have better hours, etc.

I WANTED MORE INSIGHT into his decision, so we sat down in a private room, and I asked why he was leaving. Three times he told me the same well-orchestrated answer he had given the executives.

FINALLY, I LOOKED HIM IN THE EYE AND SAID, "TELL ME THE REAL REASON YOU ARE LEAVING."

He sighed and said, "Daren, do you remember teaching the S-Curve to the executive team a number of months ago." I responded, "I do."

He said, "You asked us to put a sticky note on the curve to represent where we thought we were as a company. All the executives had us in good shape, starting toward the peak but still growing and advancing."

He continued, "Do you remember that there was one sticky note that was at the very bottom of the decline as far as it could go on the paper?"

"Now that you mention it, I do."

"Well, that was mine! And when I saw all our executives living in the fantasy world that things were going great, I knew I had to leave."

THIS HIGH PERFORMER WAS CONCERNED THE ENTIRE EXECUTIVE TEAM WAS DELUSIONAL ABOUT THE CURRENT STATE OF THE COMPANY, SO HE LEFT.

ACT

DO THE S-CURVE EXERCISE WITH YOUR TEAM

GET REAL WITH YOURSELF, AND YOUR TEAM, ABOUT THE STATE OF YOUR COMPANY.[4]

CULTURAL TOOL #1
LANGUAGE - THE BRICKS AND BOARDS

THIS APPLIES TO WHAT IS COMMUNICATED AND HOW IT IS COMMUNICATED. ESTABLISHING A COHERENT AND CONSISTENT LANGUAGE WITHIN THE COMPANY IS VITAL TO ITS SUCCESS.

Be particularly aware of what I call the **"Same Words Different Dictionary"** phenomenon. Individuals can use similar language and mean vastly different things, or vice versa.

WORDS LIKE ...

"QUALITY"
"LEADERSHIP"
"EXCELLENCE"

... CAN MEAN A WIDE RANGE OF THINGS TO DIFFERENT PEOPLE IN THE COMPANY.

WHEN I TRAIN COMPANY LEADERS, I ASK PEOPLE TO GET A PICTURE IN THEIR MIND OF THE WORD "VACATION". PEOPLE'S PERSONAL IMAGES DIFFER WIDELY.

WHAT DOES VACATION MEAN TO YOU?

Sitting on a beach with a drink in your hand?

Starting early in the morning exploring the sites and attractions of an exotic locale and collapsing in bed late at night?

Relaxing in a cabin in the woods with no digital access and a stack of books beside you?

Hiking great distances while exploring nature?

Being trapped in a car with a bunch of cranky children?

AS YOU CAN SEE, ONE WORD CAN MEAN COUNTLESS THINGS TO DIFFERENT PEOPLE.

MISUNDERSTANDINGS HAPPEN DAILY IN COMPANIES WITH VAGUE PHRASES LIKE ...

"I WANT THIS DONE RIGHT."

"I NEED THIS SOON."

"YOU HAVE A BAD ATTITUDE."

And many more inane adages that could have WILDLY different interpretations in the absence of clarification, details, or a previously established shared language.

A MULTITUDE OF PROBLEMS ARE SOLVED WITH CLEAR COMMUNICATION.

I teach a communication course called **Social Styles** to small businesses and Fortune 500 companies. It is the single most powerful communication model I have come across.

COMPANY LANGUAGE NEEDS A REFRESH

Company language hearkens back to an outdated business world full of command, control, and hierarchical management structures.

IN A CONTEMPORARY WORLD, ANTIQUATED COMMUNICATION METHODS STIFLE PRODUCTIVITY, CREATE DISENGAGEMENT, AND GENERATE UNNECESSARY AND DAMAGING BARRIERS.

REPLACE TERMS LIKE
Boss
Employees
Headcount
Assets
Managers
Supervisors
Chief
Rank and File
Etc...

TRY INSTEAD
Team Members
Partners
Product
Specialists
Facilitators
Advocates
Leaders

FOR EXAMPLE, INSTEAD OF SAYING,

"Every **LEVEL** of our organization..."

SAY,

"Every **PART** of our organization..."

LEVEL

implies a structural hierarchy and communicates that some components of the organization are "higher" and more important than other components.

PART

does not imply hierarchy and equally values all contributions to the company's goal.[5]

C2

CRAFT IT...

DEFAULT CULTURES happen by accident.
They emerge as a convoluted mess.

DESIGNED CULTURES HAPPEN ON PURPOSE.

THEY ARE DESIGNED INTENTIONALLY FOR MAXIMUM EFFICIENCY.

T H I N K

**IS YOUR COMPANY CULTURE
DEFAULT CULTURE OR DESIGNED CULTURE?**

Define in **three sentences** or less your
current business **Culture**.

DEFAULT CULTURES

HERE ARE SOME COMMON DEFAULT CULTURES
THAT DO **NOT** PERFORM AT A PEAK LEVEL.

COBBLED CULTURE

COBBLED CULTURES piecemeal together a Culture with no real rhyme or reason. These Cultures throw band-aids over issues that go much deeper, hang on to outdated policies, and just keep haphazardly adding elements as they grow.

MY WIFE ELISE AND I WERE IN SAN ANTONIO WHEN WE SAW A BEAUTIFUL OLD BUILDING WITH ORNATE DOORS, WINDOWS, AND TRIM.

WE LOOKED UP and saw a modern high rise that had been built on top of, and on each side of, the much older building. It was a brilliant solution to preserve a historic building while taking advantage of the prime real estate on which it sat. It was quite the architectural feat.

HOWEVER this is NOT a good solution when architecting a Culture. Stacking new Cultures on top of old Cultures lacks consistency and creates an unstable foundation for the company.

A **cobbled** Culture is a **chaotic** Culture

COPYCAT CULTURE

COPYCAT CULTURE takes successful Company Cultures behaviors and mimics them to try and attain success.

For example > Google

does this, so
we should also **do it.**

CULTURE IS ONE AREA WHERE ONE SIZE DOES NOT FIT ALL.

Just because it works for XYZ Company, does not mean it fits your objectives, vision, and mission.

IT IS CERTAINLY acceptable to borrow from successful companies who exhibit Culture behaviors that fit your organization but be careful about trying to copy someone else's Culture completely.

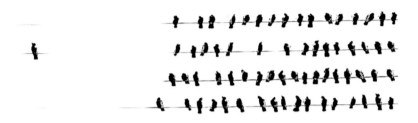

CONSENSUS CULTURE

CONSENSUS CULTURE has everything happens based on unilateral agreement.

THIS MEANS THERE *ARE NO ...* — OUTLIER IDEAS — REMARKABLE RISK TAKERS — INDUSTRY LEADING INNOVATIONS

... because they all get **averaged out.**

When you **Opt for the average...** YOU end up being average.

CALCIFIED CULTURE

CALCIFIED CULTURES are stuck in a time warp and wouldn't dream of changing what worked 50 years ago.

ON VERY RARE OCCASION, THIS SERVES THE COMPANY WELL, BUT MOST OF THE TIME IT ENDS UP BEING A BEACHED WHALE NEEDING DESPERATELY TO LEARN HOW TO # "SWIM IN THE NEW OCEAN." [6]

6: Learn more about calcified cultures and how to fix them in my book, Unbeach Your Company: Learning to Swim in the New Ocean.

(MONO) CHROMATIC CULTURE

(MONO) CHROMATIC CULTURE
Look around the office or boardroom. Does everyone look like you, think like you, dress like you?

IF SO, YOU HAVE A MONOCHROMATIC CULTURE.

Thriving cultures in the new world are accessible to many **different** people with a **wide range** of **experiences.**

COVER YOUR A** CULTURE

COVER YOUR A CULTURE** are built around the lowest common denominator. These companies employ the "Don't Get Fired Or Make Waves," unwritten rule.

IN A CULTURE WHERE EVERYONE IS TRYING TO PROTECT THEMSELVES, EVERYBODY EVENTUALLY GOES DOWN WITH THE SHIP.

IN ORDER TO AVOID THESE DEFAULT CULTURES, YOU MUST: CRAFT YOUR OWN.

CRAFTED CULTURES

TO ARCHITECT YOUR COMPANY CULTURE, CRAFT YOUR CULTURE BASED ON THE CORE OBJECTIVES, NEEDS, VALUES, PRODUCTS, AND PEOPLE IN YOUR COMPANY.

CULTURAL TOOL #2
VALUES - THE NAILS

Endless possibilities.™

ENRON, which went bankrupt from fraud, and whose leaders went to jail, had these values displayed in their lobby:

INTEGRITY | COMMUNICATION | RESPECT | EXELLENCE

(These values were not, however, what was really valued at Enron)

NETFLIX

Source: "Netflix's famous culture deck"

WHAT DOES OUR COMPANY VALUE?

- Working Hard OR **WORKING SMART**
- Authority OR **INFLUENCE**
- Individual Contribution OR **COLLABORATION**
- Firefighting OR **PROACTIVE FORESIGHT**
- Taking Risks OR **AVOIDING RISKS**
- Going Fast OR **GOING SLOW**

T H I N K

DOES YOUR COMPANY CULTURE REFLECT THESE VALUES?

WRITE DOWN the first **5 things** that come to mind that you believe are valued and rewarded at your company either directly or indirectly. No filtering. **Have 5 other people do the same thing and compare the lists.**

THIS CONCEPT SHOWS UP EVERYWHERE

MY BROTHER CRAIG has traveled the world filming philanthropy work. His work is exampled in his show on PBS called "The Good Road," as well as his book about his experiences called, *Confessions of a Philanthropologist*.

In America, Craig wore an earring that brought disapproving glances from the ultra-conservative organization he worked for at the time. Later, Craig traveled to a village in the heart of Africa for work.

One of the village chiefs approached Craig's colleague and said,

"Your friend must be a very wise man."

The colleague was confused and asked,

"Why do you say that?"

"BECAUSE IN OUR VILLAGE YOU DON'T RECEIVE YOUR SYMBOLIC EARRING UNTIL YOU ARE VERY OLD AND WISE. FOR SUCH A YOUNG MAN TO HAVE RECEIVED HIS EARRING ALREADY, WELL ... HE MUST BE VERY KNOWLEDGEABLE."

What is not valued in one Company Culture, may be greatly valued in another. Identify what your company truly values.

WHAT IS YOUR MISSION?
DO YOUR PARTNERS SHARE THESE VALUES?
DOES YOUR CULTURE REFLECT THESE VALUES?

You want your team to be comprised of people who believe in your company's mission and values. If you center your Culture around your values, your team will naturally gravitate towards this Culture because they already believe in it.

Daren Martin changed the trajectory of our company. We would not be where we are today without Daren Martin.

Bruce Sammis, CEO, Lockton

WHAT BROUGHT ABOUT THE INCREDIBLE PRAISE FROM THE TOP PERFORMER OF THIS COMPANY?

We were sitting in his office years ago and he was upset about the fact that a competitor had created a new market strategy/product line.

HE WAS CONCERNED that his team wasn't catching up to the competitor fast enough by offering their customers a similar product.

Finally, I said...

Bruce, the question I would ask is, what kind of company do we need to create to be the ones coming up with the new idea in the first place?

THE ONE QUESTION PROMPTED A
WHOLE NEW VISION FOR THE COMPANY
THAT DROVE TREMENDOUS GROWTH
IN THE COMING YEARS.

GREAT INSIGHTS OCCUR WHEN YOU ASK THE RIGHT
QUESTIONS. HERE ARE A FEW QUESTIONS TO CONSIDER
WHEN CRAFTING YOUR COMPANY CULTURE.

Get a pen and a **piece of paper** and **write down** your **responses**.

OUR COMPANY CULTURE IS CRAFTED ACCORDING TO OUR...
PURPOSE

PRODUCT
What are we trying to **produce**?
VISION
Where are we trying to **go**?
VALUES
What is **important** to us?
BAM
What is our **Business Actionable Mantra?**[7]

PEOPLE

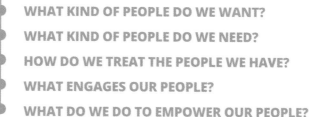

- WHAT KIND OF PEOPLE DO WE WANT?
- WHAT KIND OF PEOPLE DO WE NEED?
- HOW DO WE TREAT THE PEOPLE WE HAVE?
- WHAT ENGAGES OUR PEOPLE?
- WHAT DO WE DO TO EMPOWER OUR PEOPLE?

PROCESS

What are our ...

- **PRINCIPLES?**
- **EDICTS?**
- **GUIDELINES?**
- **MODUS OPERANDI?**
- **TOOLS?**

T H I N K

KEY QUESTIONS TO CONSIDER

01 What do we want to value? What do we actually value?

02 How do we interact with and treat our team members?

How do we want to interact with and treat our team members?

03 What does it feel like to work here?

How do we want it to feel like to work here?

04 What do we wish we didn't tolerate?

05 What do we actually not tolerate?

06 What makes us excited to come to work?

How are we advancing and growing each other as individuals?

How are we actively advancing the company?

08 What does it mean to be a part of this group?

CATER LUNCH AND HOLD 3-5 MEETINGS (WHICH WILL BE ROUGHLY 1.5 HOURS) WITH 8-10 PEOPLE (FOR EACH MEETING) FROM A WIDE RANGE OF DIVERSE RESPONSIBILITIES IN THE COMPANY.

Have a **conversation** with your **team members** to begin **outlining** the **particulars** of your **Desired Culture**.

> You can't solve a problem with the same level of thinking that created it in the first place.

Albert Einstein

DEFINE THE DESIRED CULTURE:

Arrange cross-functional teams to define the kind of Culture that would be ideal for all perspectives.

Focus on outcomes, such as:

"WE WANT INTERACTION AND COLLABORATION AMONG OUR WORK TEAMS,"

NOT particulars,

"WE NEED FREE SNACKS IN THE BREAK ROOM."

NEW INFORMATION IS NEEDED to elevate your Culture. Have members research one Culture online and report what they discover. Implement the things your members are excited by.

PICK GREAT CULTURE COMPANIES with great Cultures and learn from their practices. Read books or articles on Culture. Define the Culture in a present-tense series of statements, using phrasing like, **"We are ..."**

A CULTURE SNAPSHOT
ADDRESSING THE FOLLOWING:

(BVA: Behaviors, Values, Attitudes)

BEHAVIORS
HOW WE ACT

VALUES
WHAT IS IMPORTANT TO US

ATTITUDES
OUR PREDISPOSITION TO THINGS

OUR COMPANY CULTURE BEHAVIORS

These are the core behaviors that exemplify our Culture.

E.g., *We leave things and people better than we found them.*

OUR COMPANY CULTURE VALUES

These are shared values among the group.

E.g., *Everyone deserves to be heard.*

OUR COMPANY CULTURE ATTITUDES

These are the core attitudes that reflect our Culture.

E.g., *We seek first to understand and then to be understood (Stephen Covey).*

*Please Note: This process requires several iterations before it begins to truly take shape.

BONUS

C

Clarity

ON THE BEHAVIORS, VALUES, AND ATTITUDES
that make up your Culture is vital to making the Culture a reality and
not simply something on paper (what I call a "Paper Culture").
Make it concise, clear, and actionable.

A
LEADER
STATING

"We care about the environment," sounds great but it doesn't direct your team members actions.

"We find and implement ways to significantly reduce our ecological footprint on a daily basis," is much clearer and will drive behavior.

"We put our customers first," can create major confusion within different scenarios. Contrast it with "We treat everyone in our company, including our customers and vendors, like we would a best friend or cherished family member."

BREAD DELIVERY GUY

I WAS WALKING DOWN THE STREET EARLY ONE MORNING WHEN A MAN CALLED OUT ASKING IF I COULD HELP HIM.

He was trying to deliver bread to a recently opened restaurant but the door was locked and he could not get the attention of the staff. We banged on the door together and finally one person looked at us from the kitchen. They ignored us. Another person held up their hand indicating that they will be with us in 5 minutes.

SOMEONE came lumbering to the door, frustrated
at the interruption, and in that moment,
I developed my maxim.

THE WAY YOU TREAT
ANYBODY

IS THE WAY YOU TREAT
EVERYBODY![8]

These individuals treated a bread delivery man as though he was a second-class citizen who had all the time in the world to serve them.

But ANY individual deserves
FIRST-CLASS
treatment.

8: You can learn more about this maxim in my book Unbeach Your Company: Learning to Swim in the New Ocean where I explain that Beached companies "alienate others with a class mentality." 9* If it is not beginning to take shape, reach out to me at Daren@DarenMartin.com

C3

CAST IT...

" **GET THE RIGHT PEOPLE ON THE BUS.**
JIM COLLINS

T H I N K

MUCH LIKE A SPORTS TEAM is only as good as its players, your Company Culture is only as good as your people.
A chain is only as good as its weakest link and a company is only as good as its least engaged team member.

THE MEMBERS OF YOUR TEAM WILL MAKE THE
DIFFERENCE BETWEEN YOUR COMPANY SUCKING
AND YOUR COMPANY SOARING.

BUSINESS IS A

GAME

JUST LIKE ANY OTHER GAME, you play to win.

To **win**, you need the **best players** on the field.

SOME COMPANIES HAVE TOP TALENT WORKING
THERE BUT DON'T RECOGNIZE, EMPOWER,
SUPPORT, OR DEVELOP THEM.

NOT ONLY DO YOU NEED THE BEST PLAYERS

but they need to play at their **fullest potential**!

We often talk about getting
the **"right"** people on the bus
but we seldom ask
who the **"right"** people **are...**

HERE IS A QUICK HIT GUIDELINE
OF
PEOPLE YOU WANT
VS.
PEOPLE YOU DON'T WANT!

Wrong PEOPLE

LORDERS - As I said in the prequel to this book, *A Company of Owners* - Command and control is dead. Put a fork in it already. You want servant leaders not dictators, or "Let them eat cake" executives and managers.

LAGGERS - These folks wait to be told what to do. I was at a company where an individual was fired. I asked why. Their manager said, "If you asked Ken to go get an elephant, he would go get you an elephant. But he would never go get an elephant on his own.

LIMITED - I overheard a lady on an elevator at a conference say, "I have been doing this for 20 years. They can't teach me anything!" If I had been this person's CEO, they would have been out of a job before they arrived at their floor.

Right PEOPLE

LEADERS - You want true leaders who inspire, encourage, and develop other people. These are people others love to follow and for whom they have massive respect.

LOADERS - These are people who are constantly rolling up their sleeves and jumping into to help with the work vs. barking orders from a distance while they sit in their ivory tower. The ones who walk the talk.

LEARNERS - Learners are earners! They read, they grow, they are constantly honing their skills and learning new things. They learn about every aspect of their company's business, whether they are directly involved or not. Nellson Burns, who was head of IT at a successful oil and gas company, could clearly explain the refining process though it was not his true area of focus.

THE ARROGANCE OF ONE LEADER COSTS THE COMPANY BILLIONS OF DOLLARS

HAL SPERLICH was a respected engineer at the Ford Motor Company. Sperlich was an idea guy. One of his ideas was to build a small, light, great looking car that would be appealing to younger people and the young at heart. When Hal and Ford President, Lee Iacocca approached Henry Ford II with the idea, he didn't want to spend the money on it. By one account of the event, Iaccoca and Sperlich badgered Ford so much that he finally approved the new vehicle concept by saying, **"You can have your G*ddamn car!"**

THE MUSTANG WAS A HUGE SUCCESS.

YOU WOULD THINK that this would make Ford interested in Sperlich's other ideas, but later Sperlich had a vision that Ford ignored again. Sperlich had the idea for a vehicle that could replace the clunky station wagon and become the new family-friendly vehicle. It would need to be spacious and comfortable, which would require front-wheel drive so that he could save the space taken up by the drive train, and be just small enough to fit in the average garage.

WHEN LEE IACOCCA (still President of Ford) and Hal shared their vision for this vehicle, Ford hated the idea and was concerned, yet again, with finances. In advocating for his idea, Sperlich pushed Ford too far and he told Iacocca to, **"Go fire Sperlich!"** which Iacocca dutifully did.

SPERLICH LEFT FORD and went straight to Chrysler. Once there he came up with the K-Car which helped the then-failing Chrysler company flourish. Iacocca, after also being fired by Ford, joined Sperlich at Chrysler as the CEO and they developed Hal's vision for a new family vehicle: the minivan.

SPERLICH WAS LARGELY RESPONSIBLE FOR SAVING CHRYSLER.

CHRYSLER SOLD 500,000 MINIVANS a year, for many years to come. It took other automotive companies, including Ford, YEARS to finally produce their own version.

FORD HAD A GENIUS WORKING FOR HIM BUT HIS ARROGANCE WOULDN'T ALLOW HIM TO SEE IT OR SUPPORT IT.[10*]

10* Thanks to Guy Kawasaki for making me aware of this great story in his fantastic book Rules for Revolutionaries.

HIRING PROCESS GENIUS

A PROMINENT FAST-FOOD CHAIN has an interesting hiring practice. The interviewer "accidentally" knocks a stack of papers off the desk. If the interviewee jumps down to help pick up the papers, they are still in the game. If they sit there and watch the interviewer pick up the papers, they are not hired.

THEY WANT TEAM MEMBERS TO AS I CALL IT, "**GO TO THE BALL!**"

THEY HIRE PEOPLE WHO EXEMPLIFY THE CHARACTERISTICS THEY PRIORITIZE WITHIN THEIR CULTURE.

WHAT IS YOUR COMPANY'S P P RATIO

THREE KINDS OF PEOPLE IN YOUR COMPANY'S P RATIO

PROMOTERS

These team members are passionate about the company and sing its praises to whomever will listen. I told a lady who had a long career with Apple as a creative, that I am not an Apple customer of the company and their products - I am a raving fan. She said at Apple, they call people like me Evangelists.

These people are actively and loudly verbal about how much they don't like the company. They have a myriad of complaints, justified or not, and loving sharing them with others. I have had numerous times where a cashier or employee of a company would gripe about how bad the company was the whole time while they were "serving" me.

PEEVED

HINT: GREAT COMPANY CULTURES ARE HEAVY ON THE PROMOTER SIDE, LIGHT ON THE PASSIVE SIDE, AND PEEVED TEAM MEMBERS ARE AN ABSOLUTE RARITY IF THEY EXIST AT ALL.

These team members are Switzerland. They are neutral and don't really promote the company or disparage it. Typically they are there for a paycheck and don't really get too invested or excited one way or the other.

PASSIVE

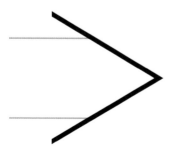

Great COMPANIES...

ATTRACT
TOP TALENT

01 Can I see myself here?

02 Do I LOVE what I see?

03 Will they invest in me?

04 Will I grow here?

05 Do they need what I have?

06 Do they have the things I need?

07 Do I like the people here?

LIKE ATTRACTS LIKE.

To attract **owners** to your company, your company must **exemplify the qualities that you want to see** to prospective team members.

RETAIN
TOP TALENT

HOW WOULD YOUR CURRENT TEAM MEMBERS ANSWER THESE QUESTIONS?

01 Am I growing?

02 Am I valued?

03 Am I proud to be here?

04 Am I contributing?

05 Am I challenged?

06 Am I loving it?

You can attract the quality team members you want, but **if the hidden Culture does not back up the spoken Culture, you will lose your owners** to a company that values what that worker brings to the table.

T H I N K

DOES MY HIRING PRACTICE ALIGN WITH THE CULTURE
I AM TRYING TO CRAFT AT MY COMPANY?

Sit down with the head of hiring at your company and **develop
a new process** (or refine your current one) that ensures you are
**identifying the qualities that you need within your Culture
in every candidate.**

THE SOONER YOU REFINE YOUR PROCESS,
THE SOONER YOU BEGIN BUILDING A QUALIFIED TEAM.

DOES YOUR COMPANY ADDRESS THE

THREE S'S?

SECURE

BASIC NEEDS ARE MET

This includes things like a livable salary and benefits. (These items are often expected by workers, but if you don't have them, you will feel the negative effects through lower engagement.)

SAFE

EVERYONE IS FREE TO BE THEMSELVES

Free to share ideas. Free to express ideological differences and still share the company's goals.

SUPPORTED

ENCOURAGED TO PURSUE YOUR PASSIONS & INTERESTS

Encouraged to use your unique skills, abilities, and insights. Encouraged to bring your brain not just your brawn.

BONUS HIRING QUESTIONS!

DO YOU WANT TO DO A JOB OR MAKE A DIFFERENCE?

HINT: THEY SHOULD WANT TO MAKE A DIFFERENCE!

ASKING THE RIGHT QUESTIONS FINDS THE RIGHT OWNERS.

CULTURAL TOOL #3

CURRENCY – THE SCREWDRIVERS, HAMMERS, AND DRILLS

DEPENDENT ON CONTEXT, currency can be many different things. In prison, cigarettes are currency. When my dad was a kid, marbles and comic books were currency.

CURRENCY does not have to be a tangible object; it can be an exchange of ideas, behaviors, or status.

EACH COMPANY POSSESSES THEIR OWN UNIQUE CURRENCIES.

THESE CAN INCLUDE ...

- Being buddies with the boss
- Being the top sales leader
- Flying under the radar
- Being a bully
- Great communication skills
- Being smart
- Being kind
- Having budget access
- Currencies are used both consciously and subconsciously during inter-company interactions.

C4

CULTIVATE IT...

THERE WAS A PERSON WHO TOLD THEIR SIGNIFICANT OTHER,

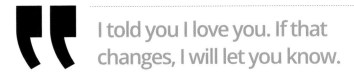

> I told you I love you. If that changes, I will let you know.

IN A ROMANTIC RELATIONSHIP thought patterns like this are obviously an issue. This attitude would also be an issue in your company. If you want ideas to stick at a company, then you need to make them sticky.[11] This means they need to be stated, explored, repeated, and implemented in every part of the company.

DON'T: **"Set it and forget it."**

DO: **Return to your mission, mantra, vision, and purpose regularly. Evaluate your progress. Refine as you grow.**

11: Read Made to Stick by Chip and Dan Heath.

YOUR COMPANY CULTURE

WHAT YOU PURPORT to value and live on a daily basis, must influence every part of your organization. You want your Company Culture to shine through and direct every behavior, including...

- Your hiring and firing practices
- Physical environment including layout and decor
- Policies
- Review process
- Meetings
- Customer interactions
- Vendor and contractor interactions
- Interoffice communications
- Customer interactions
- And every other area

Not only must you make it **"sticky,"** but you also want it **living** and **breathing**.

JUST LIKE IN A PETRI DISH, CULTURES ARE ALIVE!

EPIGENETICS

Lab researchers now have the ability to take
3 identical stem cells with the **same DNA** and put
them in **separate petri dishes.**

Depending on what is added to the stem cells in the different
petri dishes, each one can develop a different product:
one bone, one skin, and one muscle.

COMPANY CULTURE IS THE SAME AS THE PETRI DISH.
PLACE THE SAME PERSON IN THREE DIFFERENT CULTURES
AND THEY ARE APT TO REACT DIFFERENTLY IN EACH ONE.

Think of your team members as individual stem cells that will grow into your company. Healthy companies are comprised of healthy organisms and a healthy organism is committed to everyone's well-being. In a supportive company, each team member acts for their fellow team member's success. Any individual win is a win for the whole team.

A NON-SUPPORTIVE ENVIRONMENT CAN LEAD TO UNHEALTHY COMPETITION, A LACK OF COLLABORATION, AND ULTIMATELY, DISENGAGED EMPLOYEES.

QUESTION

IS YOUR COMPANY CULTURE

A PERFORMANCE
INCUBATOR
OR
A PERFORMANCE
DEFLATOR?

GREAT CULTURES ARE ORGANIC, NOT STATIC.

THEY ARE IN CONSTANT

FLUX

> **MANY THINGS OCCUR IN THE COURSE OF BUSINESS THAT CAN IMPACT THE CULTURE. THESE CHANGES MUST BE MET WITH WISDOM AND A COMMITMENT TO CULTURAL ALIGNMENT.**

NETFLIX

uses PowerPoint to capture their Culture mandates

(they call it their Culture Deck).

DIGITAL REPRESENTATION vs. PRINTED & POSTED ON THE WALL

allows them to make changes and improvements as they go.[12]

12: My favorite slide is the one that says, "We don't hire super intelligent jerks. It is too damaging to our team."

CREEPING CULTURES occur when no one is tending the garden, pruning the plants, or edging the shrubs. This leads to plants taking control of the garden, and no one wanting to dive in and get their hands dirty because of the huge undertaking it would be.

CULTIVATED CULTURES reflect how much time and attention has been given to how every area of the business impacts and amplifies the engagement, satisfaction, and performance of the team. This leads to an engaged team that is excited to dig into the process every day.

> **BECAUSE CULTURES NATURALLY GROW,**
> **YOU CAN END UP WITH A CREEPING CULTURE**
> **OR A CULTIVATED CULTURE.**

MINOR CHANGES THAT CAN IMPACT THE CULTURE

- A few hires or fires
- Policy changes
- Upturns or downturns in the market
- Growing complacency
- Halting reinvention
- Poisonous or low performing team members

MAJOR CHANGES THAT CAN IMPACT THE CULTURE

- Merger or acquisition
- CEO or influencer change
- Dramatic market shift
- Major geographic move

T H I N K

WHAT ARE MINOR OR MAJOR DIFFERENCES THAT HAVE CAUSED SHIFTS AT YOUR COMPANY?

I WAS WORKING WITH A COMPANY that acquired two large facilities a mile apart from each other. The two Cultures were radically different. The first acquisition was of a publicly held company whose executives had been threatening the operation with a shut down for the previous five years. The workforce was beat down, tired, and happy to be acquired.

SEVERAL OF THE RETAINED KEY LEADERS had a management style that I call, "management by screaming and yelling obscenities at people." They even used phrases like, "GO PUT A BOOT ON THEIR NECK."

THE FACILITY that was acquired 6 months later was radically different. It was a privately-owned family company with a really "nice" Culture. Here, the owners showed up at holidays to pass out bonus checks, shook everyones' hand, and actively tried to connect with the team.

TO THE PEOPLE AT THIS FAMILY COMPANY, THE ACQUISITION WAS PERCEIVED AS A HOSTILE TAKEOVER.

AFTER THE COMPANY ACQUIRED these two "assets" they decided to merge their operations together under one management team. Because of being acquired first, the "pit bull" managers from the first acquisition retained more control over these newly acquired assets.[13]

SEEING A TRAIN WRECK COMING, I suggested that one of the senior members of the company include "change management" in the transition period. He replied, "No, let's just throw them together and let them work it out."

THREE YEARS LATER, after major issues and countless anonymous letters to corporate HR about how bad things were, the acquiring company decided to make some changes and I was brought in.

IT WASN'T UNTIL A FEW KEY REMOVALS AND A SHIFT IN MANAGEMENT PHILOSOPHY THAT THEY STARTED TO SEE PROGRESS IN THE AREAS THAT REALLY MATTERED TO THEIR SUCCESS. THIS CHANGE IN SUCCESS INCLUDED A DRAMATIC CHANGE IN THEIR PROFITABILITY.

13: I would strongly contend that a much better practice would have been to pick the best talent from both operations.

WHEN THEY PUT
my recommendation
as head of operations in
place, the plant changed
almost overnight. In fact,
there were posters up
around the plant with
a picture of the new
manager and the word,
"HOPE" on it, á la Barack
Obama.

BLAKE ARRINGTON

IF the Culture had been a key area of focus **AND** they had channeled resources in this direction, **THEN** they would have witnessed exponential gains much earlier on.

IN A MERGER OR ACQUISITION?

MAKE CULTURE AN AFTERTHOUGHT! **=** **GUARANTEED PATH TO FAILURE**

CONTRAST THE EARLIER ACCOUNT OF FORD WITH THE INCREDIBLE STORY OF HOW WD-40 DRAMATICALLY INCREASED THEIR REVENUE BY FOCUSING ON COMPANY CULTURE.

Garry Ridge came to WD-40 in 2007 right before the 2008 crash. In the toughest of circumstances, he was able to take the company to fantastic new places.

HOW DID HE DO THAT?

BY MAKING COMPANY CULTURE **HIS TOP PRIORITY.**[14]

CULTURAL TOOL #4
BELIEFS – THE PAINT

Like civilizations throughout history,
companies have both spoken and unspoken
expectations and beliefs that drive behavior.

SOME BELIEFS
BORDER ON DOWNRIGHT
SUPERSTITION.

Company beliefs can be heard in phrases like

The last time somebody tried that it didn't work out so well.

BELIEFS ARE OFTEN ARTICULATED IN AN "IF - THEN" STRUCTURE.

- **IF** Rajeev approves of you, **THEN** you have it made.
- **IF** you don't want to be fired, **THEN** I wouldn't question the bosses' decision on this.
- **IF** you want a promotion, **THEN** you better figure out how to get here earlier in the morning.
- **IF** you want a raise, **THEN** you better speak up more in meetings.

Healthy beliefs **UNIFY A TEAM,**
provide team members with a **roadmap,**
and ultimately **create success**.

HEALTHY BELIEFS
LOOK LIKE

- Everyone having the opportunity to be successful in your company.
- Everyone supporting their teammates' growth and advancement.
- Shared passion about your mission as a company.

T H I N K

Do these **beliefs** reflect the **Culture**
I want to **create?**

Anonymously poll a variety of employees from different parts
of your company on their beliefs about the company.

What do their beliefs tell you about the company?[15]

$
NET - NET

- ✓ Not having your Culture where it needs to be is costing you massive amounts of $$$.
- ✓ Companies that get their Culture right can realize an increase of 756% to their net profitability.
- ✓ Great Company Cultures attract and keep the best of the best performers.
- ✓ Great Company Cultures outperform bad Cultures on every conceivable metric.
- ✓ Creating a great Culture is a leader's #1 priority.

THE
FINISHED
PRODUCT

Creating a great Culture is NOT hard.
It just takes time, attention, **and** know-how.

I GAVE YOU THE KNOW-HOW, but the other two are up to you. Use your strengths, draw on your resources, and empower your team to become an active part of the process.

WITH INTENTIONAL LANGUAGE, unifying values, and powerful beliefs, you will be able to radically change your employees into owners and your business into the company you always knew it could be.

REMEMBER, YOU CAN ALWAYS COME BACK TO THIS BOOK AND REMIND YOURSELF OF THE KEY CONCEPTS YOU LEARNED.

If you need help, or just want to shorten the process, **my team and I are more than happy to help.**

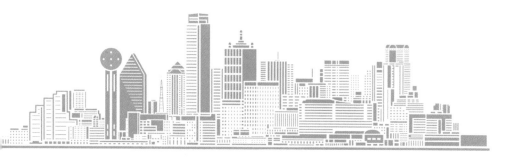

WELCOME TO YOUR
NEW COMPANY CULTURE

Daren Martin, PhD
THE CULTURE ARCHITECT
Global Speaker & Author

My name is Dr. Daren Martin and I am The Culture Architect and an Evolutionary. My goal is to Evolve Companies to make them higher performing, more profitable, and more engaging.

I produce highly engaging, meaningful, and actionable content that transforms the way people work, the way people experience life, and maximizes engagement in companies and organizations around the world.

I do this through writing easily digestible and high-impact books and material, producing dynamic videos, providing powerful keynotes, creating highly sought-after training, and advising companies.

THE CULTURE ARCHITECT DEFINED

Culture Architects design Company Cultures that maximize the desired vision, purpose, and outcomes of a particular company or organization.

CULTURE ARCHITECTS focus on enhancing the experience, enjoyment, empowerment, and engagement of the people involved, including team members, business partners, customers, and others.

ALL MY BOOKS REPRESENT A COMPREHENSIVE SYSTEM TO MAKE YOUR COMPANY GREAT!

A COMPANY OF OWNERS: Maximizing Employee Engagement

Unpacks secrets and methods to creating a fully engaged company of owners.

UNBEACH YOUR COMPANY: Learning to Swim in the New Ocean

Announces with a mega-phone what is broken in many companies and how to fix it.

ARCHITECTING A COMPANY OF OWNERS: Company Culture by Design

Is the how to companion to A Company of Owners. It maps out the four essential steps to creating a great Culture.

NAME: Create a Winning Company Culture

Presents a groundbreaking new paradigm for understanding and creating Company Culture.

BizBuzzBang outlines how to know what your true business is, how to create Buzz, and the importance of bringing the Bang.

Whiteboard: Business Models that Inspire Action

Empowers leaders with business models and tools to thrive.

Think/WOW describes how you incorporate an Owner Mentality into every aspect of your customer service so that

you can create an Outstanding experience for both internal and external customers.

The Sink: Radical Transformation with One Small Change

Inspires an entire company to continuous improvement and care.

The Tale of Three Coaches

Is a little teaching tale about the power of collaborative leadership over command and control.

Real Change Now: Company Change Mastery

A how to guide from driving change and becoming a true Change Master.

OR **SCAN** TO **VISIT**

VISIT THE DAREN MARTIN BOOK STORE

www.darenmartin.com